THE ESSENTIAL COLLECTION

MENDELSSOHN

GOLD

Published by:
Chester Music Limited,
8/9 Frith Street, London W1D 3JB, England.

Exclusive Distributors:
Music Sales Limited,
Distribution Centre, Newmarket Road, Bury St Edmunds, Suffolk IP33 3YB, England.
Music Sales Corporation,
257 Park Avenue South, New York, NY10010, United States of America.
Music Sales Pty Limited,
120 Rothschild Avenue, Rosebery, NSW 2018, Australia.

Order No. CH68640
ISBN 1-84449-592-2
This book © Copyright 2004 by Chester Music.

Compiled by Quentin Thomas.
Music engraved by Note-orious Productions Limited.

Printed in the United Kingdom.

Your Guarantee of Quality:
As publishers, we strive to produce every book to the highest commercial standards.
The music has been freshly engraved and carefully designed to minimise
awkward page turns to make playing from it a real pleasure.
Particular care has been given to specifying acid-free, neutral-sized
paper made from pulps which have not been elemental chlorine bleached.
This pulp is from farmed sustainable forests and was produced
with special regard for the environment.
Throughout, the printing and binding have been planned to ensure a sturdy,
attractive publication which should give years of enjoyment.
If your copy fails to meet our high standards, please inform us and we will gladly replace it.

www.musicsales.com

CHESTER MUSIC
part of the Music Sales Group

London/New York/Paris/Sydney/Copenhagen/Berlin/Madrid/Tokyo

Felix Mendelssohn

Felix Mendelssohn-Bartholdy was born in Hamburg in 1809 into a well-to-do Jewish family. The family moved to Berlin when Mendelssohn was very young, where he was lucky enough to be brought up within a strong cultural and intellectual atmosphere. Many writers and thinkers met at his parents' house, and his precocious musical talent was quickly recognised and nurtured. From a young age he was respected as a pianist, conductor and composer. His works were rooted in the elegance and order of Classical forms yet nevertheless embodied the Romantic principles of heightened expression and the depiction of ideas and stories. He wrote music across all the main genres, but his orchestral music is notable for its inspired and effective orchestration.

Mendelssohn travelled widely throughout his life and received encouragement from many other composers. He composed thirteen string symphonies in his early teens and in 1825, at only seventeen years of age, he wrote his famous *Octet for Strings*. The work is vivid and exciting and is regarded as a masterpiece of chamber music. The opening section of the first movement has been transcribed for this album.

A year later Mendelssohn composed his famous Overture to *A Midsummer Night's Dream*. In 1843 Mendelssohn used some of the themes from the Overture to write thirteen interludes of incidental music for use during the play. Two of these interludes are included in this album, including the famous *Wedding March*.

Mendelssohn's teacher, Carl Friedrich Zelter, directed the Berlin Choral Society and he introduced him to the largely forgotten works of J. S. Bach. In 1829 Zelter allowed Mendelssohn to conduct a performance of Bach's *St. Matthew Passion*, heralding the start of a long-term Bach revival. Later that same year, Mendelssohn made his first visit to England and Scotland. He recorded his impressions in jottings and sketches, as he did a year later in Italy.

These journeys provided the inspiration for some of his best-known works, including the *Scottish Symphony* (1842) and the *Fingal's Cave Overture (Hebrides)* (1830), which both include depictions of sea and storm. In his *Italian Symphony* (1833) he tried to put across the warmth and vitality of Italy with a bold and energetic first movement and a Czech pilgrims' song in the second. Movements from all these works have been transcribed for this album.

In 1833 Mendelssohn became the city music director of Düsseldorf, where he began a revival of Handel's music. The influence of Handel's style of writing for the chorus is evident in Mendelssohn's own oratorios, *St. Paul* (1836) and *Elijah*, written for performance at the Birmingham Music Festival of 1846, where it was a huge success. Two movements from this enduringly popular oratorio are included in this album, as well as a transcription of *Hear My Prayer*, a hymn for choir and soprano solo which includes the famous melody 'O for the wings of a dove'.

In 1835 he took the prestigious post of conductor of the Leipzig Gewandhaus orchestra, where his work was admired and respected. He improved standards and continued to champion Bach and Handel, as well as promoting new composers and conducting his own works. He married Cécile Jeanrenaud in 1837, with whom he had five children. He continued to visit England, making ten journeys in all, where he was extremely popular as a conductor, loved by choral societies and acquainted with Queen Victoria and Prince Albert.

In 1843 Mendelssohn founded the Leipzig Conservatoire, a leading centre of musical studies to this day, and in 1844 he wrote the first great Romantic violin concerto for the leader of the Gewandhaus orchestra. The second movement is included here, a songlike, rather touching Andante.

Although Mendelssohn achieved fame as a conductor he was also a virtuoso pianist and he wrote music for piano throughout his life. The first movement of his *Sonata in B♭ major*, and the second movement of his *Piano Concerto in G minor* is included here, as is a selection of his popular *Songs Without Words*, short lyrical pieces depicting a mood. Although some of them may be regarded as rather over-sentimental nowadays, most are distinguished examples of Romantic miniatures and have stood the test of time. His works for organ formed only a small part of his output. The sonatas are made up of individual Voluntaries that were grouped together later. Two examples of these are included in this album.

By the mid-1840s Mendelssohn had reached a high point, admired across Europe, holder of a prestigious post and happily married. Maybe the freshness and openness of his youthful compositions had gone, but many of his later works, e.g. the *Violin Concerto* and *Elijah*, achieved instant acclaim. However, on his return from his last visit to England in the spring of 1847 he learned that his sister Fanny, to whom he had been very close, had died. He immediately wrote a string quartet in the dark key of F minor, after which he fell ill and died in November of the same year.

Kate Bradley
April 2004

Fingal's Cave Overture 'Hebrides'

Composed by Felix Mendelssohn

Arranged by Quentin Thomas

Allegro moderato

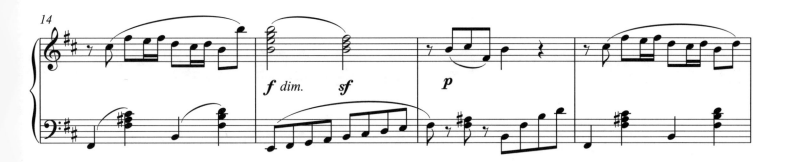

Consolation
(Song Without Words Book 2, Op.30, No.3)
Composed by Felix Mendelssohn

Adagio non troppo

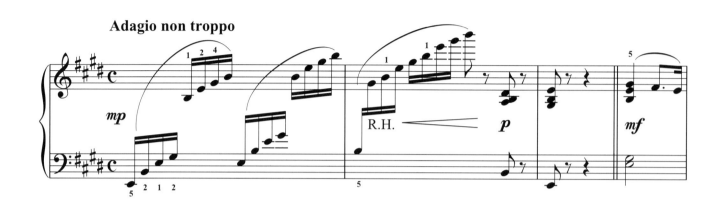

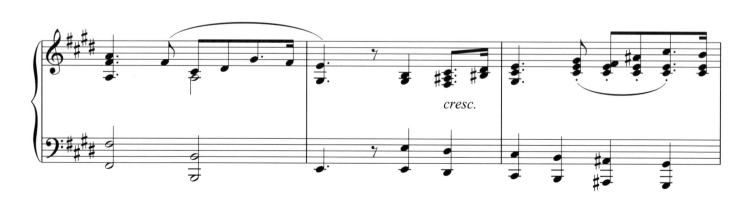

11

He, Watching Over Israel

(from Elijah)

Composed by Felix Mendelssohn

Arranged by Quentin Thomas

Hark! The Herald Angels Sing

Composed by Felix Mendelssohn

Arranged by Quentin Thomas

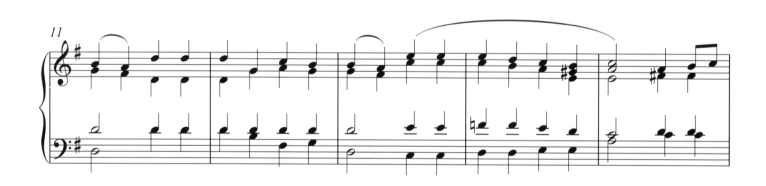

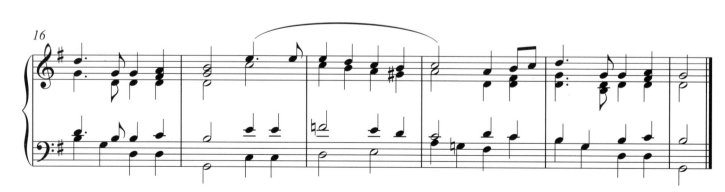

I Waited For The Lord
(from Lobgesang)

Composed by Felix Mendelssohn

Arranged by Quentin Thomas

Lift Thine Eyes
(from Elijah)

Composed by Felix Mendelssohn

Arranged by Quentin Thomas

Andante con moto

March Of The Priests

(from Athalie)

Composed by Felix Mendelssohn

23

Nocturne
(from Midsummer Night's Dream)
Composed by Felix Mendelssohn

O For The Wings Of A Dove

(from Hear My Prayer–Psalm 55)

Composed by Felix Mendelssohn

Arranged by Quentin Thomas

Octet For Strings
(1st Movement: Allegro moderato ma con fuoco)

Composed by Felix Mendelssohn

Arranged by Quentin Thomas

Allegro moderato ma con fuoco

Organ Sonata No.2 in C minor
(2nd Movement: Adagio)

Composed by Felix Mendelssohn

Arranged by Quentin Thomas

Organ Sonata No.3 in A major
(1st Movement: Con moto maestoso)

Composed by Felix Mendelssohn

Arranged by Quentin Thomas

Piano Sonata in B♭ major

(1st Movement: Allegro vivace)

Composed by Felix Mendelssohn

Piano Concerto No.1 in G minor
(2nd Movement: Andante)

Composed by Felix Mendelssohn

Arranged by Quentin Thomas

Seven Characteristic Pieces:
No.1 Snaft und mit Empfindung

(Quietly, with feeling)

Composed by Felix Mendelssohn

Seven Characteristic Pieces:
No.6 Sehnsüchtig
(With longing)

Composed by Felix Mendelssohn

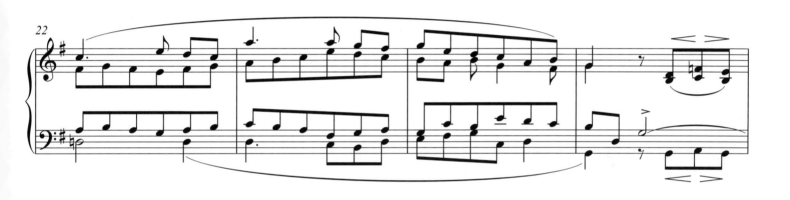

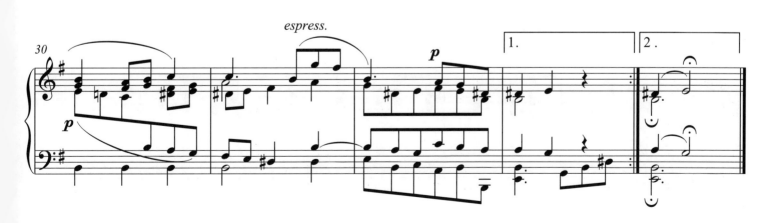

Six Pieces For Children, Op.72: No.1 Allegro non troppo

Composed by Felix Mendelssohn

Allegro non troppo

Six Pieces For Children, Op.72:
No.3 Allegretto

Composed by Felix Mendelssohn

Six Pieces For Children, Op.72: No.5 Allegro assai

Composed by Felix Mendelssohn

Allegro assai

61

Spring Song
(Song Without Words Book 5, Op.62, No.6)

Composed by Felix Mendelssohn

Sweet Remembrance
(Song Without Words Book 1, Op.19, No.1)

Composed by Felix Mendelssohn

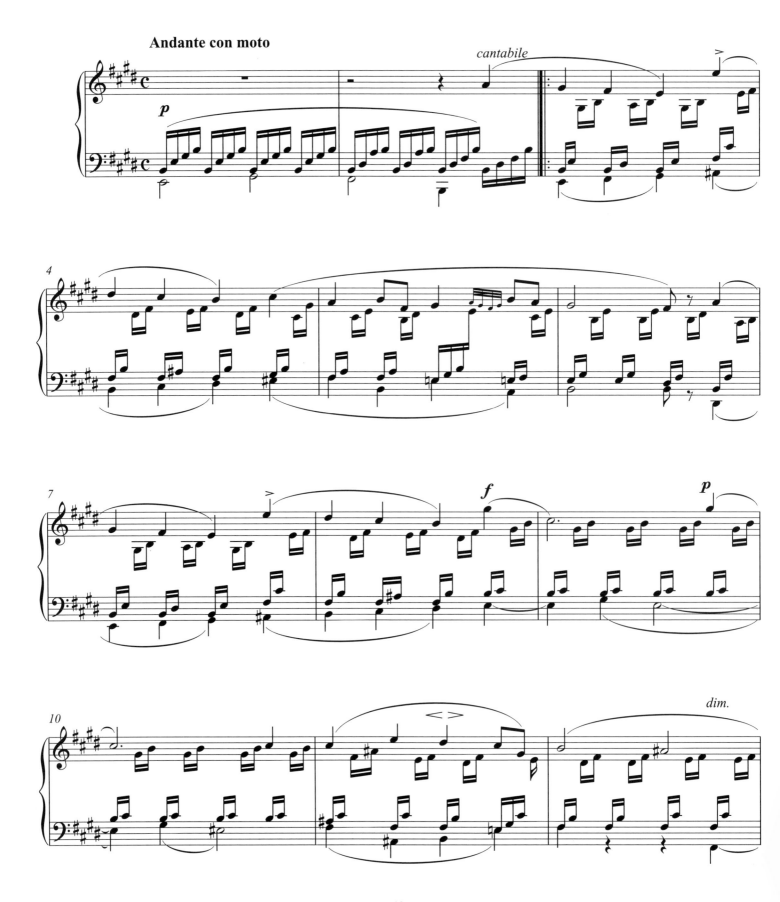

Symphony No.3 in A 'The Scottish'
(1st Movement: Introduction & Allegro)

Composed by Felix Mendelssohn

Arranged by Quentin Thomas

Symphony No.3 in A 'The Scottish'

(3rd Movement: Adagio)

Composed by Felix Mendelssohn

Arranged by Quentin Thomas

Symphony No.4 in A 'The Italian'
(1st Movement: Allegro Vivace)

Composed by Felix Mendelssohn

Arranged by Quentin Thomas

Allegro vivace

Symphony No.4 in A 'The Italian'
(2nd Movement: Andante con moto)

Composed by Felix Mendelssohn

Arranged by Quentin Thomas

Violin Concerto in E minor
(2nd Movement: Andante)

Composed by Felix Mendelssohn

Venetian Boat-Song No.1

(Song Without Words Book 1, Op.19, No.6)

Composed by Felix Mendelssohn

Wedding March
(from Midsummer Night's Dream)

Composed by Felix Mendelssohn

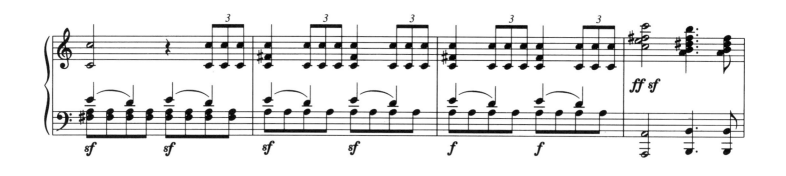

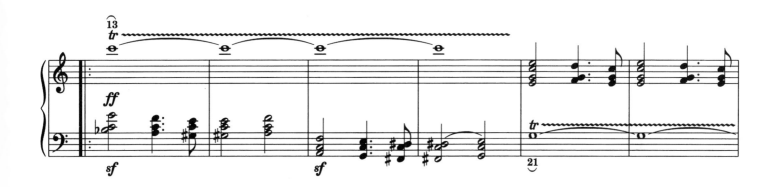

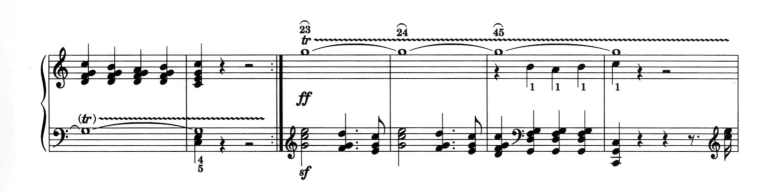

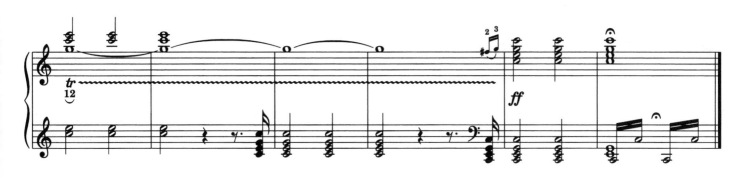

Regrets
(Song Without Words Book 1, Op.19, No.2)
Composed by Felix Mendelssohn